Dear Sister…
A Book of Poetry and Conversation

A. FRIEND

Poetry by Vicki Lichter

ISBN: 0692282912
ISBN-13: 978-0692282915

DEDICATION

This book is dedicated to every woman who's walked this planet and experienced any form of heartbreak and hardship. That means all of us… Through the sharing of our experiences, we can help one another heal and move forward. We can be a source of uplift and empowerment for each other. With every beam of love and light in my heart I dedicate this book to you all, my Dear Sisters…

CONTENTS

ACKNOWLEDGMENTS

To the Almighty Creator who chose me to be an empath, healer, and artist I am forever grateful. Thank you for entrusting me with the wisdom to help others come into themselves.

I must acknowledge the amazing poetry of Vicki Lichter. Each poem you find in this book was written by her. This is how Vicki helps to release the baggage of her herstory -- through writing poetry which tells its tale. I thank Vicki for her dedication and hard work writing these 13 poems, baring her soul, and allowing me to shed light from a different perspective onto her writings.

I am deeply grateful for the support and love of my husband Khalid and my children Dakarai and Nassir. It is with their encouragement and willingness to allow me the freedom to write that this volume is possible.

And I cannot forget the support of Stephanie Chapman, published author of 6 novels including the *These Women* trilogy, who was the soft voice in my ear gently encouraging me to stay on task and nudging me forward.

Lastly, a HUGE thank you goes to Tori Amos, co-founder of RAINN (www.rainn.org), who gave us her blessing on this volume and sealed it with an "Amazing Book!" autograph. The work that Tori does in the field of helping survivors to rebuild and thrive is simply amazing. I aspire to have this book as well as future works be one of the resources that Tori, RAINN, and other organizations can use to assist those in need of healing.

Thank you all for your contributions to ensuring that this work was birthed.

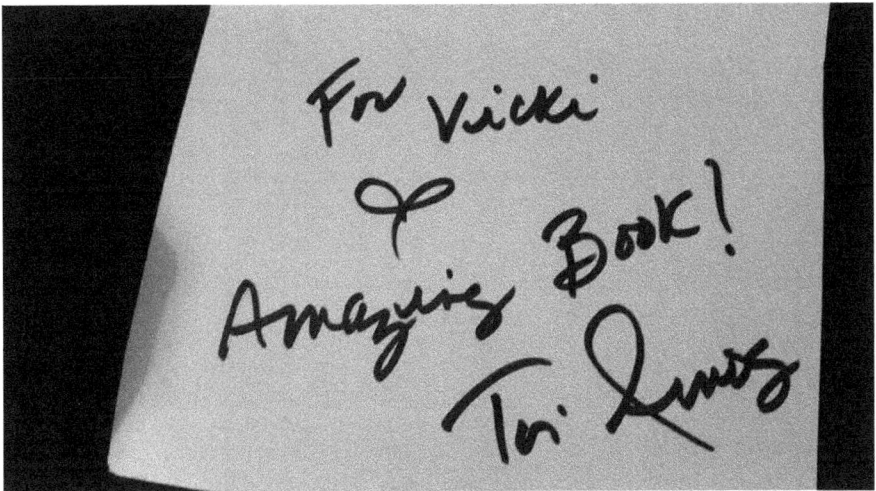

Autograph from Tori Amos (co-founder of RAINN)
Given to the poet, Vicki Lichter, after Tori received and read a
special handcrafted copy of Dear Sister… handmade by A. Friend as
a gift for Ms. Amos.

S.U.R.V.I.V.O.R.

Sometimes you think you can't go on
Unburdening this load is just too much
Re-opening wounds you've spent a lifetime concealing
Very deep are these wounds, so deep they have scarred your soul
It will take time, but you will heal
Victorious you will rise, greater than the sum of your pain
Overcoming your past by taking control of your future
Remember who you are, for you are a SURVIVOR.

Dear Sister,

You are a Survivor! Yes -- **Y.O.U.!** I know right now, baby girl, that you are probably thinking that you are not. That you are just someone's punching bag, be it physical punching or mental jabs. But know that you are a Survivor!

How so? Because right now you are sitting there reading this. That means that you are alive -- the most important state to be in. The second most important state for you to be in is in a state of inquiry, which you are demonstrating by reading this book. You are inquiring with yourself how to overcome, how to move out of this chamber of your life and get to the next path. The path of freedom and no more pain...

And you are on the right track. You have taken the first small step of many. A step into the world of words which is designed to uplift you, empower you, and share with you the wisdom of wise women throughout time. The wisdom that I have been blessed to have showered upon me I now in turn disseminate to you. That is how the Clan Mothers of Native American tradition did it -- by holding sacred women's circles and passing their knowledge onto younger generations. By holding rites of passage at various stages of girlhood, young womanhood, and womanhood. By baptizing their women with the breadth and depth of wisdom contained in centuries of sacred circles.

This is what you hold in your hands now. An invitation into the sacred circle of womanhood. And you will become an initiate of the rite of passage which moves you from victim to survivor. But not only does this volume contain the wisdom of our ancestors, it also contains the wisdom garnered through nearly a half century of my own personal experiences. Experiences which will likely resonate with you deeply. They are the same experiences of the ancestors -- but they are brought into the circumstances of the present day and therefore sometimes easier to relate to.

Your seeking resolution to your life's problems is a clear sign that you are a survivor. Those seeking comfort, uplift, and answers are empowering themselves. Those who empower themselves are seeking peace -- with Self, with life, with their circumstances... Your search for peace indicates that you have not thrown in the towel and given up. Your search for peace shows that you have not accepted your circumstances. You have not assimilated and become a resident of Victimhood. Your "hood" is Survivor Island and this book is the navigation system which will guide you from your old residence in the projects of Victimhood to the peace and tranquility of the streets of Survivor Island. Are you packed and ready? Let's Go!

How To Use This Book

This book is not linear. It wasn't written to be read from cover-to-cover straight through like a novel, although that is certainly an option if you are so called. It is designed such that you can go to whatever poem or love letter from me which calls to you.

Yes -- these are my love letters to my sisters. Written from my heart with the intention to uplift and empower you. I share my experiences and give you a different outlook by showing you there is a blessing in the lessons of life, but also that you don't have to wallow in hurt and despair because of your current circumstances. This is done in hopes that you can avoid some of the hurt I have endured by being wiser to the woes of women.

Or you may be experiencing a specific difficulty which one of the love letters specifically speaks to. Jump to that letter! Read the words of the poem and allow the beams of light in the letter to reflect and reframe. This will help you to see the other side of your story -- the side that resides in a positive light…

The exercises are designed to help you release the baggage, reframe the negative thoughts and change your thought processes into those which uplift and empower rather than those which degrade and belittle. Do some or all -- the choice is yours. I encourage you, however, to do the exercises because they will help you to integrate the messages. For a more indepth look at how to complete the exercises, there are videos available showing how to create the art journal pages from the exercises in this book. Visit **www.dear-sister.transcendental-wings.com** for full-length videos on some of the exercises found here.

Points To Ponder

I want you to think about the words in the poem *Survivor*. If you were like me when you were reading it, you were shaking your head yes and agreeing with all of the feelings and thoughts that the first part of the poem speaks of. What I want to you to process, however, are the thoughts and feelings that came up for you when you reached the end of the poem:

> *"Victorious you will rise, greater than the sum of your pain*
> *Overcoming your past by taking control of your future*
> *Remember who you are, for you are a SURVIVOR.*

What comes up for you when you read these lines? Do you believe this rings true for you? Do they make you feel uncomfortable thinking about taking the steps necessary to change your situation and thereby change your life? Do you see that you are making the first steps through working through this book to "overcome your past by taking control of your future"? Do you feel -- do you KNOW that you are a Survivor?

Alchemical Art Journaling Activity

Time to pull out your journals! For this activity, you will need:
A pen
White gesso or white acrylic paint
Paintbrush
Various colored markers of your choice
A candle to light
Soft drumming sounds (preferably no words)
The most important thing you'll need is an OPEN MIND!

Allow the process to work through you. It may seem silly or unnecessary but do it anyway -- especially if you think it's not going to help. Don't make judgments on the process or what result you end up with. Just breathe into the exercise and allow the result to integrate into your psyche and become one with you, uplifting and empowering you.

Purge

Put on your drumming music to play softly in the background. In your journal, open to a blank page, and dump all of your thoughts onto the page. Everything: the good, the bad, and the ugly. Get it all down. Don't worry about it being neat and nice and pretty -- it won't be hanging around for long... Every feeling in your body needs to be written on this one sheet of paper in your journal. If you run out of space, do what's called "overwriting" -- when you get to the bottom of the page, turn your book 90 degrees and keep writing on top of the words you wrote first. **It is not necessary to be able to read the words!** I just need you to get them out, sincerely and fully. Give yourself a <u>minimum</u> of 15 minutes to just sit and write, but take as much time as you need to get all of the muck and junk out and onto the page.

Meditation Moment

Once you are finished writing, light your candle and close your eyes. Allow your breathing to fall into its natural cadence. Sit back and relax into your seat, getting as comfortable as possible. Allow the soft drum sounds to wash over you, removing any leftover dust from your writing session. As you continue breathing with your eyes closed, imagine yourself walking down a path toward a doorway in the distance. You can see that there is a door, but there is not much else you can make out about it. Look around you. What other signs or symbols do you see? Are there birds and flowers and insects? Are there shapes or other symbols you see, even if you don't quite know what they are? Continue walking and looking around and taking in all of the sights and sounds and smells. As you draw nearer to the doorway, there is a flash of light above the threshold as a word is emblazoned above the entryway. As the fire burns the word into the wooden structure, you take in the appearance of the door. What does it look like? Is it ornate and heavily embellished like the doors to an ancient cathedral? Or is it a simple door with simple shapes and colors? Take in its every detail and then lift your eyes above the threshold and behold the word that has been etched there for you. What is the word? Now that you have been given direction, turn and begin to make your way back down the path toward your point of origin. As you walk, continue to take in the scenery, making note of anything that is significant to you. When you reach the start of your path, take a deep breath in and release it as you say "Sweet Release." Now open your eyes. Welcome back!

Paint

Now, take out that white gesso/paint and paint over the words on the page that you wrote earlier. Cover them all up so that you cannot see any of the writing. As you are doing this, thank those thoughts and situations for their lessons and then Let. Them. Go! They have served their purpose in your life and now it's time for you to release them into the Universe so that they can go on to take their message to the next one in need. Release them now and do not allow them back into your head, into your mind space. Do not give them free rent in your head! Every landlord has to evict non-paying tenants and the negativity on your page, which was just in your head has never paid rent and has now been evicted! Embrace the feeling of release and allow it to integrate into your heart.

Produce

Remember that journey down the path toward the doorway that you saw in the distance? Now it's time to produce that on the page! Pull out your markers and, recalling the images you saw as you journeyed, draw the door that you saw in your vision, placing the word which was emblazoned above the doorway in the same location on your picture. You do not have to be an artist to get this done -- do your best job. Only those you choose to share your journal with will see the work. It isn't about the art -- it is about the process, the purging, and the healing that is garnered through the process.

Integrate

Integration is the process of taking the good out of all of this and incorporating it into your being to heal you and make you better. The word which appeared above your doorway in the visioning is a call to you for action. It is a reminder for you, a beacon of light in the darkness to help guide you where you need to be. No one but you can manifest your destiny and this word is just a small part of the beginning of that manifestation.

On the back of your picture, write the word in large letters in the center of the page. Sit with it for a while and let it speak to you. Close your eyes if that makes it easier for you to tune into the vibrations of the word which you were given. Listen for what it is telling you, for the guidance it is giving. When you are ready, jot down some notes about the word and its purpose in your life. When you have finished writing the meaning of the word in your life, draw the shapes and symbols that came into your vision as you were walking the path. Draw them all around the word in the middle of the page. Next to the drawing of the symbol, write down what the symbol is and what it means to you and in your life. After completing all of the symbols, look at your page and reflect upon the meaning of everything which surrounds your guide word. Integrate these things into your being and begin using them for your greater good.

You have arrived! At the beginning of your soulful journey…

ACCEPTANCE

Sometimes, Acceptance is all you have left.

When Hope has abandoned you and regret says nothing to comfort you…

When Despair lets you drown in the silence and watches as you slowly dissolve into a memory…

Acceptance is your only friend…

Acceptance of loss of what was, acceptance of what never-will-be, and finally acceptance that you deserve and will receive something even greater than what you thought you had before.

So…

Even though it's dark, and the rain's slow drizzle echoes the tears that may be streaming down your cheeks right now, don't forget…

Acceptance is always there for you…

You just need to invite her in.

Dear Sister,
Acceptance… So many of us do just that — accept what is as if that cannot be changed. What is can always be turned into what you desire, and yes – it starts with Acceptance…

But acceptance doesn't have to mean despair. Acceptance only means that you acknowledge what is in order to use that as a springboard to propel you forward to what will be. Acceptance is the review of the past in order to order your steps in the present, which thereby prepares your future for greatness.

Ordering your present steps…

That's what it's all about. Being present to THIS moment. Not dwelling on the past or looking dreamily to the future. By living in the present moment your future will form itself without your need to worry about it. Accept what was – your past – but don't dwell on it and allow it to have you skipping the present moment in hopes of what will come in the future. Create the future of your dreams by living in this moment, right here and right now.

Your future is directly dependent on your PRESENT – not your past!

Accept the past, learn the lessons delivered, integrate the lessons into your present, and live in the now. The future will unfold in its own way according to your actions RIGHT NOW – not what has already transpired and cannot be changed. Live for today. It is a gift. It is the Present! Be present to what you have right, all else will fall into the order in which it should be.

Points to Ponder

For you to experience healing, there must first come acceptance. And from acceptance, forgiveness must flourish. You cannot forgive what you haven't accepted to be…

Today, I want you to reflect upon your past. Not dwell – reflect. What are those things which need to receive the blessing of acceptance from you in order to become a blessing to you? What are those things which are waiting for your forgiveness so they can be released into the Universe to lend a teaching hand to another?

Alchemical Art Journaling Activity

For this activity, you will need:
A pen
A #10 envelope

Some writing paper
Black permanent marker (fine/medium tip)
Watercolor paints/crayons/pencils*
A piece of cardstock (12x12)
Ribbon
Adhesive

Purge

On the writing paper, I want you to write a letter to the Universe. This letter should list all those things you've come up with through your pondering which you need to accept in order that they become blessings to you. Once you've discussed what needs to be accepted, inform the Universe that you have finally learned the lessons from these teachers. Discuss with the Universe your plan for forgiveness. Then forgive yourself and those that need your forgiveness, thank the Universe for the lessons, and sign and date the letter.

Meditation Moment

Retreat to your quiet space where you can be alone with your thoughts and the light of the Divine. Get into a comfortable position, light a candle, take a sip of tea, close your eyes and relax. Allow your breath to fall into its natural rhythm. Remain relaxed with your eyes closed for 5 minutes, breathing normally and clearing your mind of any chatter. Now, open your eyes and open your journal to a blank page and begin to doodle onto the page. Don't worry about what it looks like and everybody can doodle, so don't talk yourself out of being able to accomplish this. Accept what is and doodle to *your* ability. Fill the entire page using permanent black marker. As you are doodling, reflect upon those things which you have written and released via the letter to the Universe. Accept that you have forgiven and released these things -- I mean *really* accept it. As the ink flows out of the pen, allow the pain of the past to flow out of you as well. When you have filled the page completely with doodling, give thanks for time spent in self-reflection. Welcome back!

Paint

Now that you've filled your page with sacred doodling, it's time to add color! Pull out your watercolors (*substitute acrylic paint which has been watered down to lessen the opacity if you do not have watercolors) and begin filling the page with colors that you are drawn to. Don't think too much about it, just simply let the colors flow from your center onto the page. As you are filling it with color, add additional doodles and embellishments that you are called to.

Produce

Once you've filled the page with color and the paint has dried, fold the letter you wrote earlier and insert it into the envelope. Seal it and write "Return to Sender" in big bold letters on the front of the envelope. Take the piece of cardstock and cut it into the shape of a mailbox. For a free template that you can download and use, go to http://dear-sister.transcendental-wings.com. The files on that site are free to download and use for personal use. The mailbox should be large enough to fit most of the envelope into the slot, but not so large that it covers the entire envelope. Adhere the mailbox to the page you've just created and insert the envelope. You have just returned the baggage in your life to the sender and relieved yourself of that burden! Embrace your acceptance of what was and move into the present moment to live out the rest of your journey.

Integrate

Ummmm… Do you feel the yumminess of moving from the past into the present? Do you feel the lightness, the joy of living in the here and now rather than in the past? Take these feelings, this elation that you feel now, and integrate it into your Self. Allow your being to become intoxicated with the feeling of release and forgiveness. Let it shower down upon you, filling you up to overflow.

CRUMBLE

I initially saw the handprints across her face via text message…a mess of purple and blue and hints of all the technicolor shades they would eventually fade to…the swollen lip that puffed out like an angry man's chest when he's trying to act tough…the bruises that dress her arms and inner thighs, undeniable evidence that NO was a word of nonexistence when he wanted to be intimate with his captive…I saw the vacancy in her eyes when she returned home finally free from his grasp…and when she spoke of his aggression, listless as though it was being read from a bedtime story…recounting each plotline devoid of emotion even though the whole time I knew that dam inside of her was ready to break, and release a swell of tears and heartache, yet she still managed to keep them at bay a soul who's spent a lifetime surviving by denying those emotions which would in her mind render her feeble…so over the years she became a master manipulator and played with hearts as if love were a sport and she was the MVP, used her beauty as bait and switch up masks to fit the stage…BUT now…here she is…I see her broken, shattered from the outside, battered from within…sometimes the scars that come with trauma are to remind us that no matter how hard we try to fly, we are still all Icarius, falling back to Earth just when we foolishly think our waxed on wings have made us touch sky…now some say her attack was simply karma for all the pain she caused myself and others…her vacancy of emotions gave eviction notices to the hearts who tried to love her from behind her cement walls…while letting us believe we could simply break through with bare hands as she used our blood as décor…some say she should have been more cautious…after all, people have killed for love and her hobby was igniting passion, letting it flare up then smolder out, she would extinguish it out quietly at her choosing, she should've read the warnings making sure she wasn't lighting combustible hearts…if you stand too close the explosion that follows brings only destruction…

But she says…he let me go, so now it's over…I'm moving on…I walked away…he just really likes me…and didn't want to hear no…that's all…now please, just let it go…

I take a long pause…thinking and marinating on her misguided words…and I feel the lies as she claims to still be in one piece…and so I speak. I say…stop babygirl…take a minute to look in the mirror…maybe for the very first time…really look at what has transpired…someone has done what you thought was impossible…they

12

have violated your strength, raped your sense of power…changed you undeniably in those days and hours and I don't care how far you walk, there's still a piece of you he's holding onto…that piece he stole from you in those dark days. And no matter what others may say, nobody deserves to get treated this way…my heart aches for her pain that may now never be healed. She will continue on as always, and this experience too will end up just locked down in the cellar bound and gagged along with every other disappointment, trauma, and unshed tear she refused to let too near…little does she realize that their release would be hers as well…but I guess some people need to believe they're indestructible…that the cement walls around their hearts are still erected and impenetrable…even though WE ALL know, that although they may be wearing that smile, they're just crumbling from the inside…

Dear Sister,

Crumble is only the beginning of the cycle of healing. We must first release the pain of the past and in doing so we will crumble. We will fall apart and no longer be that which we once were. But out of the darkness comes new light. We go within in order to find and integrate our shadow side, our crumbs.

As our great sister-guide and sage, Dr. Clarissa Pinkola Estes, teaches us, these crumbs are the bones which the Wise Woman gathers. Go -- gather the bones. Re-Member. Integrate the lessons of the past, the crumbs, into Self and be reborn into and of the Light. Go within and seek out that which is seeking you. As the Phoenix is reborn through fire and ash, ignite the flames of your creative passion and transform the tragedies of your past into the manifested beauty of your present. Shape your future with the actions of the here and now.

Every cycle is a season of life, of your journey. It begins with breaking down, a death of sorts, in order to be reborn anew. Awakened. Transformed. Transcended into a place of peace and harmony with Self and all that is contained within the Universe. It is through the inner shifts in our knowing, our intuition, our connection with Source and all there is. And as we cause and create that which we are called to manifest, we gather the crumbs, the bones, and we re-member. We reassemble our Self into that which we are to be in this next cycle, this next season of our lives…

So Sister, crumble. Crumble in order to be reborn. Allow the cycle of birth, life, and death to complete itself in order that you can be born anew. Crumble and begin again from the ashes of the flame lit by the light of creativity.

Points to Ponder

This poem paints a pretty grim picture of a woman who was physically and sexually abused. It reminds us of some of the ways we find ourselves acting: making excuses for someone's bad behavior, believing that it was our fault for whatever the circumstances brought into our lives, believing we deserve to go through what is being done to us, wearing the everlasting smile outwardly while inwardly the pain from the tears have caused an ocean of sadness to wash over us and stay with us for far beyond the turn of the receding of the tide…

Now ponder this: As children, we learned that "no" means "no" -- no matter the circumstances. If mom or dad or someone older than us told us no, that was the end of the discussion. We were not able to force ourselves or our opinions into the scenario as a means to get what it was that we wanted. We accepted the answer of "no" and moved on. If in your childhood "no" meant "no," why now do we believe that what has happened to us is our fault -- even after we've said "no"? This applies to any situation where someone has disrespected your wish to decline their proposal, be it an offer of food, games, drink, or sex.

It is not your fault. You didn't make him (or her) hit you. You didn't do anything to cause him (or her) to rape you. You said "no" and no means no… There is no way in this Universe that this could be your fault. No matter how smart mouthed you may have been, no matter what manner of dress you had on, no matter how you carried yourself. You are allowed to act and be exactly who you are, by your own standards and not by the standards of loved ones or society. You are uniquely you, walking your unique path. Nothing and nobody can dictate what that path has in store or where it leads but you. Therefore no one can use your decisions about your life against you, blaming you and shaming you for their actions.

Alchemical Art Journaling

For this activity, you will need:
Magazine cut-outs of cookies, various sizes
Modeling paste
Circle template
Adhesive
Small paper plate (needs to fit on page)
Acrylic paint: black, brown
Ink Sprays
Craft Sand

Purge

On each of the cookie magazine cut-outs that you have, write one word that is part of your present reality which you need to release. What are those things that need to crumble away in order that you can reassemble the crumbs and be born anew? What limitations have you placed on your being that must be removed in order for you to flower, bloom, and blossom? Write these limiting factors onto the cookies.

Once you have written them all down, tear the cookies in half and then half again (making quarters). Set these to the side. Pull out your ink sprays and spray your page with various colors to create a background. Blend the colors with water and brush to add interesting effects and dimensions. Allow the page to dry completely, or use a heat tool to dry the page thoroughly.

Now at the top of the page, adhere the cookie pieces near one another to reform the cookie onto the page. We are re-membering. Reassembling. Some pieces may touch, or overlap, or leave a slight gap. Allow the pieces to fall into their natural place and do not force the cookie back together in an attempt at perfection.

Meditation Moment

Now rest your hand upon the page, on top of the cookies. Get comfortable and close your eyes. Allow your breath to fall into its natural cadence. Quiet your mind by softly speaking these words: "I crumble in order to build anew:" repeatedly until you have released whatever thoughts that will block your light. When you have relaxed and cleared your mind, listen for the message that is hidden in the words which your hand lies upon. What is the significance of these words in your life? What are their meaning? What is the lesson to be learned from these words which you have written on this page?

When you have arrived at an answer, when you have heard the message in the meaning of these words, open your eyes. Welcome back!

Paint

Using your circle template and a scrap piece of cardstock, create several circles of various sizes using the modeling paste. Allow the paste to dry fully. Once dry, cut the circles out so that the cardstock cannot be seen. Paint the circles to make them look like cookies: chocolate chip, oatmeal raisin, macadamia nuts, etc. Once the paint is dry, write one positive word/affirmation on each cookie which directly relates to the words of release which you wrote on the magazine cookies that you cut out.

Produce

Now adhere the paper plate to the bottom of your page. Adhere the modeling paste cookies to the plate. Using the sand, create a line of "crumbles" from the magazine paper cookies to the modeling paste cookies. Allow all to dry fully.

Integrate

The paper cookies represent that which you need to release, and which you have released through this exercise. The sand represents those cookie pieces becoming cookie crumbs and falling down to the plate below, where the crumbs are reassembled to *your* liking. Think about the transformation which has taken place. Look at yourself in the mirror and see new Authentic Self shining through.

CRESCENT

The crescent shaped scar is craggy on the back of my weathered hand
A daily reminder of how deeply you claimed you loved me
And wanted to help me do my duties right
You know, just the way you liked
All because the chicken was burned
And the vegetables a bit too raw for your liking
Because you wanted me to remember to be more careful when ironing your shirt
So you gave me a reminder
Used your teeth to stamp my flesh like a post-it note
"Next time do it right"
Written in more code shaped like your mouth around my fleshy thumb mound
Colored in violet hues within the words
As I work on perfecting my mistake
As I time the chicken just right
And follow the recipe to the T so the veggies
Don't show any hint of uncooked freshness
As I re-iron your shirt for the 5th time because the crease is ½ inch too far left…again
I pray the pain will fade with my errors
But the crescent star still remains
Along with the foreboding promise
Of a full moon tonight.

Dear Sister,

The baggage of our past can cause deep scars -- be they physical or emotional. But the scars do not have to be our only memories of a situation once lived…

These scars, these wounds are what teaches us to heal. How so? Because they are a reminder for us that another path, another way is better for us.

17

They are beacons of light and wisdom beckoning us to move on from this place but use the lessons learned here to clear the path before you. These are not things to dwell on and hold you down; rather they are tidbits of the deep knowing that resides within your Self. These are the bones that Dr. Clarissa Pinkola Estes instructs us to gather and sing over. Using our "soul-voice" we are to heal these broken pieces and re-member...

It's time to get still and get quiet and hear the truth in the lessons of the past. The garbage that you are thinking -- that you need to change you and "perfect your mistakes," that you must get everything "just right" and follow the process "to a T," that you must re-do the "wrongs" you have done to others -- is just that: garbage. You are perfect in your imperfections! Your "just right" is just how YOU accomplished the task. Your following the process "to a T" is however you followed the steps and arrived at the finish line. There is no right or wrong way -- there's only YOUR WAY!

That is what this is all about. It is about embracing the you that you are right now in this moment. It is about living who you really are on the outside, out loud. It is about being the Authentic You that resides within begging to be released. The constant reminders of times past are not designed to strangle you and keep you down. They are designed to be beacons of light along your path which help prevent you from taking the wrong turn. These are tidbits of your Inner Wisdom Essence.

Points To Ponder

Not much can be learned without first suffering something unpleasant. A child learns not to touch the stove once s/he is burned by doing that very thing. A puppy learns not to pee in the house by being reprimanded, marched outside, and then confined when brought back in. A mouse learns his way through the maze to the cheese by going the wrong way many times first until it learns the right path to take... Just as those lessons weren't constructed to bring the demise of the person or animal, your life's past isn't designed to be your doom either.

> "But the crescent star still remains
> Along with the foreboding promise
> Of a full moon tonight."

It is true – with every crescent moon we know that a full moon will follow eventually. Inevitably. However, Grandmother Moon is on a intentional path which is positive. When we stay stuck knowing that a full course of hurt is certain to come our way, then we set ourselves up for the pain rather than navigate our course into the light of Grandmother Moon. If instead we realize and embrace the symbolism of the moon, it tells us we are coming into a time of illumination, as the moon is a luminary. "As a symbol of subtlety, the moon softly enfolds our attention, illuminating our psyche in a goassamer glow that is more open to esoteric impressions." (http://www.whats-your-sign.com/symbolic-moon-facts.html, August 6, 2014) In other words, we are gently lulled by the moon's luminary effect on us and by embracing the reflection of light from the sun -- the manner in which the moon is able to illuminate the sky -- we are warmed and bask in the knowledge and wisdom inherent in our connection with the Universe. It is this knowing which is our guide, this intuition, this self-reflection of the origin of ourselves which makes us whole.

Therefore, Sister, do not sit foreboding the coming of the full moon. Rather, redirect your path in order that you are aligned with the powerful and positive aspects which are initiated in the full moon's glow. Just as you sit awaiting and fearing the inevitable, you have the power within yourself to turn that inevitable occurrence into a glorious outpouring of light and self-love.

Alchemical Art Journaling

This activity is designed to be done on a full moon. Ready your supplies and wait for the night of the next full moon to complete the exercise.

Supplies
Your Journal
Iridescent Silver Paint
Cardstock
Circle Template
Payne's Gray Paint or DecoArt's Traditions Prussian Blue Hue Paint
Black Fine Tip Permanent Marker
Red Permanent Marker
Washi Tape

Purge

Sit outside under the light of the full moon. Soak in its illumination and reflect on your Self as a woman. Allow the feminine energy of the moon to wash down over you and integrate with your Self. On a blank page in your journal, write all of the baggage that came up for you when reading this poem and Dear Sister letter. What things rang through your mind's eye as a pang of pain and disappointment that is a part of your past? What shame and blame came up and washed a layer of depression and self-doubt over you? Write down what you are/were feeling when these things came up: bitterness, anger, shame, guilt... Write legibly and fairly large. Fill the entire page with your words.

Using the largest circle on your template, cut a large circle from the cardstock. The circle should be large enough to cover most of the page. Paint the circle with the iridescent silver paint and set to the side to dry. You may want to use two coats.

Meditation Moment

Now, while you wait for the paint to dry, sit comfortably in your chair. Back straight, feet flat on the ground, and your hands on your knees with your palms facing up. This is a receptive position and you are wanting to be open to receive the message(s) which are provided for you in those things from your past which you wrote about. Allow the warmth of the moon's rays to touch every part of your body from head to toe. Feel the embrace of the feminine energy as you allow your breath to fall into its natural cadence. Close your eyes and allow the energy to fill your mind, body, and soul.

On your visionary screen, pull up the image of the words you've just written in your journal. Read them to yourself again -- this time looking for the positive message within the words. Visualize a red marker and take that marker and draw a box around the words which give gratitude to the circumstances. You are looking for a sentence or phrase which speaks positively about that which is written. It is there, you just need to be still in this moment to see it. Once you have marked out the statement of gratitude, read it to yourself and allow the words to resonate with your soul.

Now, open your eyes to ready your Self for the process of giving gratitude and integrating the lessons into your heart so that you can move on past these things in peace. Welcome back!

Paint

Remember the sentence/phrase that came up for you on your visionary screen during meditation? The one you took the virtual red marker and marked out on the page? In your journal, take the red marker and put a box around all of the words which you boxed in during your visioning journey. Now, take the Payne's Gray/Prussian Blue Hue and paint over all of the other words and space on the page, leaving the red boxed words visible. Your page should be completely covered -- blocking out all the negativity you wrote -- with the exception of the red boxed words.

Produce

Next, using the black marker, write a statement of gratitude on the moon which you created with the circle and iridescent silver paint. This statement should be thanking the Divine for revealing the meaning of the lesson of circumstance in your life. Now adhere the moon to your journal page using the washi tape in such a way that the moon is a flap that can be lifted to reveal the red boxed words underneath. You are symbolically rising above those words which you have buried beneath you and bringing forth the good from the bad.

Integrate

Lastly, with a dry brush and very little paint, take the iridescent silver paint and lightly brush it from the moon onto the gray/blue page, depicting the moon's illuminating rays which are showering onto the page. Set aside and allow to dry fully. As the moon's rays have "spilled over" onto the page and caused illumination to that which was once dark, allow the message in the words and your gratitude for the lesson to be the beacon of light your soul needs to illuminate, navigate, and integrate the dark spaces. For without darkness there would be no light.

THE PAINTER

Black and blue
Violet hues
He was a painter, and I was his canvas
With a stroke of his arm,
Red would spew from my burnt-sienna
The starch white bandages shone like stars against my midnight skin
Yesterday, he painted a sunset on my eyes
The warm reds and fire oranges licked at my face from his temper
Crimson waves undulated around my eyelids each time I blinked
He was an artist, and wanted his work to remain between us
A silent conversation between the creator and the created
So I became a fashionista
Able to coordinate clothing that skillfully hid his brand of art
I knew no one would understand this work
Only I knew what each brush stroke was saying
And my body had to be his canvas, he was a painter
Black and blue and violet hues, a rainbow of his reasons
And as the paint would fade to greens and golden shades
I through his painting days were over
After all, the material he paints on is starting to wear thin
Patches of scars and small tears in the canvas
They tell a story nobody would understand, and I would rather forget
But I am his muse, his Sistine Chapel
And so I must remain, his everlasting canvas
Until the last stroke

Dear Sister,

Don't allow anyone to paint the picture of your life but you! YOU are the painter who controls the brush strokes. Take back your canvas and glaze it with the colors of a new day -- one which starts with the color of love...

Love of your Self. Love of your self-worth. Love of your right to be here, in this place at this moment. Paint the canvas black to cover the darkness, boldly stroke it with white to bring forth the light. Then pick up the colors of your soul and emblazon upon the surface the fabric of your life. Manifest the you that you want to be, the person you are authentically. You are a skilled artisan, trained in the manifestation of your dreams. Now it is time to bring them forward, into the light.

It is time to pull the underpainting forward. The foundation which began with your beginning. The other painter was there for a season, for a reason. The reason was in order to give your life depth, to fill the canvas with character and interest. Now it is time to manifest that which the underpainting has cultivated all this time. It is time to pull you forward. White wash your canvas today and begin the process of bringing forward from the darkness of the past that which was meant to remain.

Points to Ponder

The canvas of our lives is in constant flux. It is constantly changing colors, shapes, and symbols. What manifests is dependent upon that which we call into being. We have full control of the colors and brush strokes, yet we don't always realize this. We sometimes think we are not the master painters which we are and allow someone who appears stronger and more confident to paint the story of our lives. Yet it is ourselves who is truly the master.

It is time for you to come into your Self. Time for you to don the hat of "Artist" and paint your canvas your way. Don't give your paintbrush to someone else for you are the master of this masterpiece!

Alchemical Art Journaling

It is time to paint the canvas of your life. To call upon your Muse, your Inner Wisdom Essence, your Authentic Self to manifest the self-portrait that you want to show up on your canvas.

<u>Supplies</u>
11 x 14 Canvas
Charcoal (for writing on the canvas)

Black Paint
White Paint
Various Paint Colors of Your Choice
Picture of Yourself
Flower Stencils
Modeling Paste
Adhesive
Black Fine Tip Permanent Marker

Purge

Using the charcoal, write on the blank canvas your intention for this painting. Your intention should surround your desire to manifest authenticity -- your Authentic Self. Include with your intention your intent to release the hold of society/others on your life and your current action of grabbing hold of the paintbrush, becoming the master painter of your own life.

Meditation Moment

Now place your hands on your canvas and close your eyes. Feel the words, the intention of this painting on your palms. Envision this intention now being connected to your Self through your hands. Feel the sensation of it moving up your arms, across your collar bone, to and through your breast plate and settling in to your heart. Feel the warmth this brings. See the spark of flame it has ignited on the top of your heart. Allow these sensations to integrate with your Self while you are breathing in your natural rhythm.

Make note of the colors which you see before you. What is the color of your heart? What colors are the flames which spew forth from the top of your heart now that it has been ignited with your intention? What are the colors which speak to your intention? You have given your heart's desires words through intention, now give that intention the colors of your soul.

Once the colors have been manifested and noted, once the warmth of your intention has fully been integrated into your heart sparking the flame, give thanks for the power and strength to fulfill you intention. Open your eyes. Welcome back!

Paint

Now take the black paint and paint over the entire surface of the canvas, covering your intention. Paint the sides of the canvas as well, leaving no part of it white. As you paint, repeat your intention to yourself over and over and over again. Say it out loud. Allow the words to wash over you, for you will need them to bring forth your Self from the underpainting. Next, paint a large oval shape onto the canvas using the white paint. The oval should cover the entire canvas, leaving just the four corners painted black, helping to form the oval shape.

Produce

Next, adhere the picture of yourself to the center of the oval once the paint is dry. Allow the adhesive to dry so that the picture does not shift when you go to add the embellishments. Using a small amount of modeling paste and just a drop or two of paint, make a few different colors of paste. Now take your flower stencil(s) and stencil on flowers using the colored modeling paste. Place the flowers all over the canvas surrounding the picture of you. The picture should be surrounded by a deep bed of flowers in an array of colors which speak to you.

Integrate

Once the modeling paste is dry, further embellish the flowers by drawing/doodling over them with the black marker. Add veins for the leaves, dots and circles to add dimension and interest -- weave the thoughts of who you are authentically into the blooming flowers, which represent the blooming of the true you.

SHATTERED

Shattered glass and bare feet reside here
Broken love arranges in ugly mosaics
Clocks tick backwards to erase things
Be sure to escape the night
The moon steals the light often
Sunshine will help you glow alone

Dear Sister,

Again the creator being created by someone other than her own hands… You are the master artist behind the creation of you. Not society or the deadbeat that you may have in your life right now. Realize that it is you who holds the expertise to create a priceless masterpiece.

And you are priceless: There's no amount of money or any other thing of substance that can replace you. Your self-worth is far greater than the sum of your circumstances!

Shattered may be your state of mind right now, but it is those pieces of colorful glass that will be reordered -- re-membered -- to make you whole! Every bit is part and parcel of who you are, your make-up, your composition. You are the master creator behind this mosaic. It is time you built yourself a window to your world fashioned after the beauty of the ceiling and other frescoes of the Sistine Chapel…

The opportunity to rebuild is now! The pieces lie right before you as you sit and contemplate your state of disjointedness. Don't leave you standing in a state of disrepair! Order your steps, the pieces of you, into the fashion statement that you want to exude. Allow your hands and your heart to be the guide for the mosaic of your Self. Just as you decorate your room to please yourself, decorate the planes of your life to reflect the same beauty. It comes from within and you have all the tools you need to make it so.

Points to Ponder

We have all at one time or another been broken. Shattered. Be it from the battering of domestic violence or the grotesque verbiage of emotional abuse, each one of us in our lives has experienced the pain of feeling broken. But think about your favorite piece of crystal which your mother gave you on that special occasion in your life. You know, the one which somehow managed to land in the floor and break. You picked that up and put it back together didn't you? Why then would you not do the same for Self?

The Japanese have a tradition of mending the cracks in broken objects using precious metals such as gold (Kintsugi). They believe that the cracks in the masterpiece are but a window into the heart of the object and by mending it with something more valuable than itself, they are highlighting the rough patches as "an event in the life of an object rather than allowing its service to end at the time of its damage or breakage." (http://en.wikipedia.org/wiki/Kintsugi, August 7, 2014) This is what you are to do with your Self: You are to mend the cracks with the salve of your soul -- your authentic voice. You are to re-member your Self in such a way that you add more value to what was already deemed priceless. Elevate your circumstances by arranging the pieces in the order which you see fit and bring immense beauty to that which was already unspeakably gorgeous.

Alchemical Art Journaling

It's time to create our mosaic. Time to mend the cracks in our lives with the salve of our soul. For this activity, you will need the following supplies:
Paint, various colors
Gold Metallic Paint
Hot Glue Gun
Pencil and Eraser
Black Fine Tip Permanent Marker
Cardstock cut to the size of your journal page

Purge
On the blank piece of cardstock, write down those circumstances in your life that make you feel broken, shattered. You can write a simple list, or write it out in prose format. Also write down your feelings of blame and shame -- those things which you hold against yourself and allow you the feeling of disjointedness. Fill up the page with your thoughts.

Paint

Now, taking various different paint colors, paint over the words you have written. Be sure to use lots of different colors -- you are creating a mosaic and they usually enjoy a wealth of colors. It doesn't matter if some of the words show through the paint, but be sure to paint different colors all over the page. Next, rip the paper into pieces once the paint is dry. Don't make them too small, but totally dismember this writing through ripping it up.

Meditation Moment

As you are ripping up the page, settle into the knowledge that you are in the process of releasing these burdens. Close your eyes and allow your breath to fall into its natural rhythm. Allow yourself to release these things, thanking them for their message but allowing yourself to move on past what you have written. You are looking toward a new mosaic masterpiece! As you finish ripping up the page, take a deep breath in, bringing in gratitude for the lessons before you and releasing the breath with an audible "thank you for these lessons." When you are ready, open your eyes. Welcome back!

Paint

This time you are painting with adhesive. In your journal, reassemble the ripped page and paint a layer of adhesive on the front and back of the pieces, adhering them to the page and sealing the colors. Set aside and allow to dry completely.

Produce

Once the page is completely dry, take your hot glue gun and run a thin line of glue along all of the edges that have been ripped. Allow the glue to cool and harden fully. Now, with the gold metallic paint, paint over the raised glue gun lines. This is symbolic of the real gold used by the Japanese during the process of Kintsugi. You are mending the broken pieces with the precious salve of your soul. As you are completing this mending process, forgive yourself for holding onto the broken pieces too long and not re-membering them sooner.

Integrate

Once the gold paint has fully dried, use your black permanent marker to write a prayer on the page. Be creative with this part -- put a line or phrase in each section of the glued on mosaic so that when "pulled together" it becomes one cohesive prayer. Or, write one word in each section which when read creates a prayer. Just get creative with your writing and make it a personal power prayer. When done, read the prayer out loud to yourself. You should read this prayer to yourself daily in order to help you acknowledge the releasing of the past and the ushering in of the new mosaic of your life.

CHANGE

She finds herself missing the past sometimes
She will sit in the mist of the early morning and wonder where her life is going
She wonders sometimes if she will ever find her happy ending
As the sun emerges over the horizon it reminds her of the legendary phoenix
Rising anew
Every day.
Awakening to the realization the past is forever gone
And she misses it
But not for how it made her feel
Never for how it felt
She doesn't miss the pain
She doesn't miss the tears
She softly touches her skin and revels in its softness, no longer bumpy with scabs,
bruised and painful, a sensation she does not lament over
A tear streams down her face as she realizes all she misses
Is the familiarity of expectation
The pattern of the day to day
Because change can be scary
Not knowing what tomorrow will bring can frighten
Even the most impenetrable of souls
Yet in her transformation
She realizes
The knowledge of what she does NOT have to expect
What is routine for her no longer
What is now simply a part of her yesteryears
Is the greatest comfort of all

Dear Sister,

Change is difficult. It is scary. But it is necessary in order that you are able to walk the path laid out before you. Nothing ever stays the same. Think about it: You were born many years ago and were a helpless infant. Through the years, you grew and became self-sufficient. You changed and the change was for the better. It was to better you and to grow you into the person you are today. And the changes were inevitable, unable to be stopped or even slowed down. The changes happened when it happened, on the Divine schedule in which they were planned.

We are often hesitant to change. Resistant even. We long for those things, good and bad, from the past that had become our way of life until change came. We even miss the things that we had grown accustomed to -- even the hurt and pain of abusive relationships. We long to be needed by the children, the spouse, the job in ways that we were needed in the past, even though that need did not honor ourselves and left us with no time for self-care. But it is in change that we heal and grow.

When you "awaken to the realization that the past is forever gone," you will realize that your whole life lies before you -- not behind you. There will be times and circumstances that you may miss; but taking heed to the fact that change brings about something better is what your focus needs to be. It is terrifying not knowing what tomorrow will bring, not being able to depend on the same routine that had been your life. However, new routines are being developed for your life as it stands in this present moment. whether you want them to be or not. There is a Divine plan for your life and S/He has a schedule to keep! Don't make your journey harder by being resistant to the changes that are inevitable.

You can find great comfort in change if you allow it to unfold seamlessly in your life.

Points To Ponder

You have already been through years of change simply in the process of moving from infant to toddler to small child to teenager to adult. Change is inevitable. Embrace it rather than wrestle with it. Change will always win! Often a relationship you don't want to let go of makes it so you have no choice but to let go. Either the person walks out of your life or there are circumstances that cause you to walk away from them. Circumstances such as protecting your health and/or saving your life... Your job is in a constant state of flux: new HR policies, new methods for completing the same tasks you've been doing for years, new technology that improves upon production... And those changes are fairly easy for you to grasp and run with. You really have no choice -- it's change with the changes being made or lose the job that helps to support you and your family. So you change in spite of the fear associated with it.

Now transcend through the challenges of change and allow your life changes to happen as seamlessly as you've allowed your physical and job changes to happen. Doing so will allow abundant joy and peace in your life. There will be no struggle against the inevitable and things will fall naturally into place like the natural cadence of your breathing. Change can be as easy as taking a breath...

Alchemical Art Journaling

Let's create a Season of Change Wheel. For this you will need a large circle template, large enough to fill a page in your journal, and the following items:

Pencil/Eraser
Cardstock
Black Permanent Marker
Ruler
Watercolor Crayons/Pencils
Baby Wipes
Gold Metallic Paint
Adhesive

Purge

Open to a blank 2-page spread in your journal. On the left hand side, write a love letter to Change. Talk to Change about the fear you've had in the past when Change came and then tell it about your embracing Change from this point forward. Let Change know that while you were once afraid, you now understand its importance in your life and you are ready to fully embrace what lies ahead for you without worrying about what that is.

Use your best penmanship and the black permanent marker. This letter will remain in plain view for you to reflect upon.

Meditation Moment

Now that you have written your letter to Change, sit comfortably in your sacred space with your journal. Light a candle and take a sip of tea. Place your hands over what you have written and close your eyes. Relax into the natural rhythm of your breath, making sure your breaths are cleansing. Say a prayer over the letter with your intention to heed the words you have written. Thank Change for the role it plays in your life and the new understanding you have of its benefits.

Bring up your visionary screen and envision a circle. There are four parts of this circle: Winter, Spring, Summer, and Fall. These seasons represent the seasons of your life. Where does each season fall on your wheel? What colors represent the four seasons of change in your life? What words or phrases define each of these seasons? At which season of change are you now in? What other symbols are there for you to receive and add to your medicine bag?

Once you have made mental note of all of these things, thank your Season of Change Wheel for showing itself to you and explaining its message. When you are ready, open your eyes. Welcome back!

Paint

Before we paint, we must record the colors and words and phrases that came up for us during our journeying. On the right side of your 2-page spread, jot down the four seasons, the colors you saw for each, and the words and phrases that came onto your visionary screen for each using the black permanent marker. Using the watercolor crayons, color the page randomly with different colors. Try to choose colors that will look good as a backdrop to the 4 colors which came up for you depicting the 4 seasons of change. Then use a baby wipe to activate the watercolors and blend them. The words written on the page should be obscured, but still visible.

Produce

Now, cut out a large circle from cardstock using your circle template. Divide the circle into 4 quarters by drawing a vertical line which cuts the circle in half and then a horizontal line cutting the circle in half also. With your watercolor crayons, color each quarter the color for the individual season which came up for you. Use a baby wipe to activate the watercolor crayon and blend the color onto the page. Using the black permanent marker, write "Winter," "Spring," "Summer," and "Fall" into each of the sections on their appropriate color. Now, transcribe the notes you wrote in your journal onto each of the appropriate sections. For the section where you see your life currently residing, take your gold metallic paint and draw a star. Write today's date next to that star. Now adhere the circle onto the page, covering the notes you jotted down.

Integrate

The gold star that you drew on your Season of Change Wheel depicts which season you feel your life is in right now. Embrace where you are and look forward to the season that will come next in your life. When you feel changes happening, allow them to unfold naturally. Once you are comfortable in the new skin which change has brought you, go back to your wheel, draw a star in the season of life where your life is now, and write the date next to it. Continue to do this for the other seasons until you have marked the full circle of change in your life. Then, write the story of this Season of Change in your journal. Include the full details, as best you can remember. What challenges did you face in this cycle? How did you approach them? How did you resolve them? What were the lessons learned? How did your Authentic Self show herself to you during this Season's Cycle?

=

The last time you raised your voice at me, a smile skipped across my lips
Like a rose bud finally blossoming, the smile grew and grew into a laugh increasing the need for air in my diaphragm,
My bruised ribs ached and I welcomed the pain this joy
This true joy.
Your confusion showed and paralyzed you.
I could see you…calculating.
You were so sure I had gone mad.
Perhaps I did
All I knew is that fear must have evaporated from my bruises because I no longer took you seriously.
You couldn't even raise your hand to strike me as you have lost all of your power. I could see the pride draining from your eyes.
You knew I no longer respected you.
And without that it was a losing game.
I would fight for myself.
I would kill for myself.
I composed myself with my broken subservience and for the first time looked into your eyes as your equal.

Dear Sister,

You didn't think something so simple as a defiant smile would be the undoing of him/her, did you? Such a small gesture, a simple step, and look what it has netted you. You didn't have to make a huge commotion or grand stand or cause any drama. You simply smiled and it was done…

That's the power of a smile. In good times and bad a smile will always change the tide. And this small gesture is not only his/her undoing, it is yours as well. You are done being the punching bag -- be it physical or verbal. You are done not being enough for someone else when you are plenty enough for yourself. You are done playing small so s/he can feel big. And in this done-ness you are undone; you cause and create the next ripple in your life's path. You usher in change -- the change that needed to happen -- rather than wait for change to come your way. You have taken hold of the helm and made the decision to steer your own ship.

Good for you! Continue in the way you have started, with small steps. Small gestures speak volumes to what your purpose is. Grand standing and fighting out loud doesn't solve anything nor cause healing for Self. Making little changes and taking small but sure steps is all the catalyst you need for change. Change that will come sooner or later if allowed to happen in its own time. Sometimes it's necessary for us to actively effect change. When we see the writing on the wall and the rainbow on the horizon, it is sometimes necessary to act on those signs. It's still change ushering itself in on its time and terms; however, this ushering in can now happen because you've embraced the change rather than fought with it.

Something as simple as smiling rather than frowning, putting on your makeup because it makes YOU feel good about YOU, dressing for the day even if it's house cleaning and laundry day -- all these things will have a huge impact on your mind, your body, and your soul thereby bringing your Self joy. And that's really what the other person doesn't want you to have. Joy. Don't wait on him/her to provide you with joy. Give yourself the gift of joy and effect the change you need to happen in your life today!

Points to Ponder

Abusive relationships aren't about physically or mentally hurting the person. It is about control. Control of that person's mind and therefore their behavior. When you allow someone else's junk to be imposed on you, you allow them to control your actions. You won't do or you will do certain things certain ways because you know if you don't they'll be trouble with you and that person. Don't allow anyone to control you. Take the reins back and guide your own stallions. Don't allow them free rent in your mind space -- save the accommodations there for yourself! OPJ is akin to OPP and you don't want possession of either (Other People's Junk and Other People's Property). Learn to possess only that which benefits you and smile about the rest of the mess as you watch it exit into the Universe where it is called for some other purpose, some other lesson, and no longer a factor in your life.

Alchemical Art Journaling

For this exercise, all you will need is a bunch of different colored markers which you can write with, and of course your journal.

Purge
Open your journal to a blank page and turn it sideways (landscape). In the middle of the page, write a large equal sign (=). Choose 3 color markers which depict anger to you. On the left hand side of the page, list all the things which happen to you which make you feel like you are not equal.

Meditation Moment
Now get still and quiet, close your eyes and place your hands upon the page of text you have just written. Allow your breathing to fall into its natural rhythm. Clear your mind of the chatter which may be going through it. Take three deep cleansing breaths and with each breath in, breathe in peace, tranquility, and worthiness. With each breath out, breathe out chaos, bitterness, inequality. Visualize yourself as the equal to what you listed on your page. What words come up to describe you in an equal capacity? How does equality look to you? When you have contemplated what it means to be equal with the left side of your page, open your eyes. Welcome back!

Paint
On the right hand side of the equal sign, list all the things which you visualized as making you equal to the things listed on this left hand side. Choose 3 marker colors which depict freedom and happiness for you.

Produce
Now, take the markers and draw/doodle a decorative border around the page. Allow the doodles to come into the field of text without obscuring or blocking the writing.

Integrate
While you are drawing and doodling to embellish the page and put the final touches on, allow your mind to see your Self as equal to that which you feel unequal. Embrace this vision and depict its strength through the border which you doodle onto the page. Allow the strength of this inclusive box to touch upon the words on the page and in your heart.

FADING SCARS

It was the last night I would belong to you
The weight of your compression on my spirit was broken by the click of a suitcase
Packed all of my favorite things
Withdrew in cash and closed my accounts
What I hold in my hands are mine
Taking a long drive to anywhere knowing whatever meets me there will be better than
this.
Smoothing aloe vera on my skin to soothe the last scar you will ever give me
Adding honey in my tea to soothe my soul
I'm taking off my glasses and finally laying in the sunlight these bruises will fade
eventually
You will fade eventually

Dear Sister,

Yes…the scars and the memories will fade in time. And time is now what you have. Something you didn't have before you made the decision to leave… How so? Because your life was in peril each and every time you walked through that door and made the decision to stay in that relationship, to risk life and limb for what was thought to be love. But now you see how easy it was to break the grip -- the sound of the suitcase closing and locking was all that was needed. The small step of gathering up your things, your bones, and moving elsewhere to reassemble them. Some place where it is safe and where you can be reborn anew, for you have already awakened. you awakened to the truth of what was your situation and now you are causing and creating what is necessary to right the wrongs and move on.

And move on is what you have to do dear one. You must move on from the hurt and pain and take up residence where love abides. Love of Self, knowledge of self-worth, living in the present and authentically… The scars and the person will fade eventually and you will be able to live in the light, without glasses to mask the black eyes and bruises, and soak up the energy of the sun while sipping on the sweet nectar of honey sweetened tea.

Points to Ponder

How excited do you get when it's time to take vacation from work? The plans you make to go here and there and do this and that get you charged up with the energy you need to pack all of your essentials. You are looking forward to that release, that relief from knowing you don't have to go back to work for some days now. The decision to move away from an abusive relationship should give you the same feeling, the same excitement. You should readily pack your essentials and head out of the door onto new and better things. Just as the resort holds new things for you to experience and a better time than when you're at work, so too does your decision to move yourself into a better, less rocky path on your life's journey. Embrace the fading scars and look forward to the journey ahead.

Alchemical Art Journaling

This will be an exercise in learning to write with a paintbrush. You will need:

Paintbrushes
Black Paint
White Paint
Gray Paint
Glitter
Glazing Medium/Varnish

Meditation Moment

Go into your sacred space with a candle and a cuppa. Get comfortable sitting and light your candle. Nestle into your seat, take a sip, and close your eyes. Take three deep cleansing breaths, breathing in peace and acceptance and breathing out pain and solitude. Pull up your visionary screen and allow the vision of a garden to come into view before you. This is a magical garden with magical gems and precious stones which speak to you. As you explore the garden, you uncover hidden stones with words and phrases written on them. These stones are hiding because they are the stones of past bitterness and contain words and phrases which depict the scars you have come to know along your journey. Turn the stones so that you can read what's written, but do not remove them from their place. What are these words and phrases?

Now reposition the stones and gems in the manner which you found them. Ensure that you replace any dirt or growth that has begun to cover your stones. These are the stones with which you have the least connection -- you have managed to begin the process of leaving no stone unturned and addressing each of them at face value. As you place the stones back into their rightful spaces, you notice that you have managed to smear the writings. Somehow the words are starting to fade away. How does this make you feel?

Once you have placed all of the gems back into their place, walk to the nearest tree and give it a hug. Smell some of the flowers in the space. Fill your present moment with the beauty and joy and tranquility of this magical garden. When you are ready, open your eyes. Welcome back!

Paint

On a blank page in your journal, paint the page black. Be sure to cover the entire page. Set aside and allow to dry.

Produce

Using a small paintbrush and the white paint, draw "stones" all over the page. Allow this to dry. Now using a liner brush or other small paintbrush, write one word which came to you during the meditation in one stone and before it can dry, smear the word with your finger. Repeat this process for each of the stones/words that came to you. Allow this to dry fully. Next, paint each stone with glazing medium and sprinkle glitter across the words in the stones before the glazing medium dries.

Integrate

The process of smearing the words actively helps you to release this part of your past, which is fading away anyway. The glitter brightens the spot that used to be dull with pain and sadness. Take this process to heart and really lean into the process. Allow the actions of smearing and beautifying the words to integrate with your mind, body, and soul. Allow the process to heal the wounds of the past which have been limiting you. Allow the scars to fade away...

RE-INCARNATE

She is learning to live again.
Each step stronger than the last.
Spirit weakened, yet she forges ahead.
The pasts betrayal still haunt her.
Does she have strength to overcome?
Heart's telling her don't give up.

Dear Sister,

That voice that tells you "don't give up"... It is the voice of your intuition, your Inner Wisdom Essence. Often we don't heed this little voice and we should. A woman's intuition is unmatched and deserves to be the voice of reason for us. Sadly, we look to external signs to guide our lives. We really need to be taking a long hard look within.

There is always a rebuilding after the storm. That's where you are now -- in the rebuilding phase where you are learning to live again. The energy here is that you are moving on, and the key is that you look ahead to where you are headed and not look back. I am not saying not to continue to nurse the wounds. I'm not saying forget the past -- that is an impossibility. What I am saying is that now that you are strong enough to move on, keep it moving...

Your heart is telling you not to give up! Heed the calling of your heart!! You have made it this far, through whatever it is that your path has led you to and through, now is not the time to give up. If you are knocked down 4 times then you must get up 5 times! Your spirit will become stronger the further along this new path that you tread. Don't allow the haunts of the past to make you falter, slip, or become stuck in quicksand. Your heart is beating a strong drum, the drumming of your awakening and transformation.

March to the beat of your own drum -- your heart!

Points to Ponder

Do you remember the parable of the gold digger who dug and dug and dug and dug and finally became discouraged enough that he stopped digging -- 3 feet from the treasure of gold he sought? Had he simply stuck to the calling of his heart, he would have reached the gold in short order. This is exactly what we do to ourselves when the going gets rough. We begin to doubt Self, believe the whisperings of low self-worth that are in our head, and then we give up. We choose to stay in situations that aren't ideal rather than forge ahead through difficulty and turmoil to the pristine path. Don't be the gold digger and give up 3 feet from the prize! Rebuke the negative, limiting, self-talk through positive affirmations and daily gratitude. Being grateful for what is right in your life can cause and create the strength you need to continue the journey ahead of you, not wallow in the one you left behind.

Alchemical Art Journaling

This time we are going to reach down within and pull out our inner child. You will need the following supplies:

Your Journal
A Box of Crayons
Pencil/Eraser

Purge

On a blank page in your journal, write down all of the things that oppose your heart's calling of "don't give up." Those limiting thoughts and beliefs of why you can't possibly go on is what we are seeking to release here. Write down those things which keep you stuck still and/or looking to the past rather than forging ahead.

Meditation Moment

Now retreat to your sacred space if you are not already there. If you have one, wrap yourself in a sacred prayer shawl. Lean into the protection that the shawl offers you while you are in a vulnerable state of meditation and prayer. Close your eyes and allow your breath to fall into its natural cadence. Clear your mind of any chatter that may hinder your time meditating. Pull up your visionary screen and allow a meadow to come up before you. In that meadow is a path that leads on into infinity. Look around you. What is it that you see? Are there birds and trees and flowers? What animals and insects are present in this meadow? What are the colors which grace the landscape? What does that path which you stand at the start of look like? Is it weed covered and grown over? Is it a golden magical path? Is it the yellow brick road? Feel the energy of this meadow -- the trees, birds, insects and animals all have something to share with you. They are sharing the energy of their strength in the face of difficulty. Forests are constantly being cleared to make way for people, putting these natural treasures in peril. Listen to the message of strength that they are telling you. What is it that they are saying? How are they empowering you to forge your path ahead without concern for what's happened in the past? Once you have finished sitting in conversation with this magical meadow and receiving the wisdom therein, open your eyes. Welcome back!

Produce

Using your pencil, draw a picture of the meadow from your meditation on the page of limiting thoughts you just wrote. Draw right over the words you've written, as the drawing will become a covering -- a protection from the limits of the past just as the prayer shawl was your protection while vulnerable during meditation and prayer. Include all of the bits of nature that came up for you -- trees, flowers, animals, insects.

Paint

Now with your crayons, color your picture in with the colors of the meadow which also revealed themselves to you. There is meaning in the colors which were most prominently in your vision.

Integrate

The exercise above is a visual aid to integrating past lessons with the present. We need to cover those things from the past with a layer of protection which lies between us and it in order for us to move forward. Just as the crayons did not fully cover the words written -- they simply obscured them and pushed them into a place where they could no longer affect what we were doing in the present -- so too should we cover ourselves in protection through gratitude giving. By being thankful and consciously giving gratitude for the lessons of the past, for what we do have in the present, we are able to fully integrate those lessons without allowing them access to limit us.

LAST BREATH

I'll give you my last breath.
Exhaling your name from my chest.
I'd never leave you to drown.
You've swam through tides of disappointment.
Life's undertows constantly pulling you under.
Never give up, you're a survivor.

Dear Sister,

As women, we love hard. We love our children so much we'd give our lives for them. We love our (wo)men so much that sadly sometimes we actually do give our lives for them -- not by choice though... But when we heed the voice of intuition, then we survive. Remember to love yourself first! That means that you will give your last breath for your Self; that you will exhale *your* name from your chest; that you won't allow your Self to drown. You have swam through tides of disappointment and have beaten the undertow which time and time again attempts to pull you down. Now nor ever is the time to give up!

The energy you expend loving someone who is clearly not loving you back should be expended on loving your Self. On realizing for your Self the trials and tribulations you have been through yet you are still here, alive and kicking. Realize that you are still here for a purpose and that purpose isn't to be someone's verbal or physical punching bag. You must realize that you are needed, that you are worthy. You've fought this long and come this far with the peril of being pulled under. Never give up. You are a survivor.

Points to Ponder

There are many arenas that tell you to "pay/put yourself first." That's one of the first, most basic principles in money management: pay yourself first. It's no different in life. You cannot be valuable to anyone else if you don't first value yourself. Throw yourself a life jacket and save yourself from drowning through breathing for yourself first. Even during an airplane's safety instructions prior to taking off they instruct you to put the face mask on YOURSELF FIRST. Save your Self first…

Alchemical Art Journaling

Time to pull out the floatation device! For this, you will need:
Your Journal
Modeling Paste
Acrylic Paint
Cardstock
Paper (copy weight/20 lb)
Adhesive
Black Permanent Marker (Fine/Medium Tip)
Miniature Bottle (can be purchased from a craft store)
E6000 Adhesive
Sandpaper
Pencil/Eraser

Purge

Cut strips of paper that will fit into the miniature bottle. On each of these strips, write a word or phrase that describes those things which are limiting you right now. Is there something you fear? Write it down. Do you feel unworthy? Write that down. Whatever thoughts that are unbecoming write on the strips of paper. Once you have filled the bottle with these thoughts, glue the cap on the bottle using the E6000 adhesive. You have sealed these limitations into a bottle and effectively prevented them from being a limitation to you again.

Meditation Moment

Nestle into a comfortable chair in your sacred space. Take a sip of tea and light a candle. Begin releasing the chatter in your mind as you prepare to look within. Now close your eyes and breathe deeply. Take slow, deep, cleansing breaths. Pull up your visionary screen and allow the vision of yourself on a deserted island, your boat at the shore in disrepair, to come into view. Now envision the bottle with the self-limiting thoughts you wrote in the first part of this exercise. Take a hold of it in your hands, whisper quietly "Thank you for the lessons which have caused a new turn in my path to come into being." Walk to the shore and release the bottle into the sea of water before you. Now stand back and watch as the waves carry the bottle far far away. As the bottle drifts away, open your heart to the new day you have caused for yourself. Turn away from the sea just as the bottle disappears from sight. Before you a path has been cleared. Stand at the start of this new path in your life and say a prayer to the Divine which calls to your being a survivor, which gives thanks for the lessons of the past, and which opens up the possibilities that lie before you on this path. When you finish your prayer and when you are ready, open your eyes. Welcome back!

Paint

On a blank page in your journal, paint a clear sky, with the sun shining bright. Add a few soft clouds to help show off the day.

Produce

Using some of the modeling paste, add a drop of blue-green paint and mix together with the paste. You are looking to make the paste appear the color of the sea. Now spread the colored modeling paste onto the bottom of the page, making it look like the sea. Tear a strip of sand paper and add some E6000 adhesive to the back. Press the sandpaper strip into the modeling paste on the page at the edge of the paste to create the look of a sandy beach shore. Set this to the side and allow to dry fully. This may take overnight.

Draw a person on the cardstock, making sure that it is drawn such that it can be cut out. Paint/color the image. Using your adhesive, adhere the cut-out to the page in one corner, with the person standing on the beach. Draw and cut out a boat which has been shipwrecked on shore. Adhere this to the page as well, near the person who is standing on the shore. Lastly, adhere the miniature bottle to the page on the opposite side from where the person is standing. Adhere it into the sea -- not on the shore. Remember, these are the limiting beliefs that you have set a float.

On the opposite page, write down the prayer that you made at the end of the meditation. Don't fret if you don't remember exactly what you said -- put down what feels right in this moment. This prayer is your floatation device. Use it to get to the shore of the new day and new path in your life.

Integrate

You have bottled up the limiting beliefs which were once holding you back. You have embraced the dawning of a new day and a new path. The limiting beliefs are on their way to be lost at sea forever. Remember this. you do not have to wallow in the past. Gather the bones, pray over them, integrate the lessons into Self, and set a sail all else.

THINGS WE LOST IN THE FIRE

Identity
We lost ourselves
In the fire
All the things that made us into We
Everything that gives us the pieces we needed
To keep me and you whole
Separately
And yet completely
United
We watched it burn that day
Together rose in the ashes
Memories of days gone we no longer cherish them in delicate hands
But instead we grasp them roughly in the moment then throw them to the embers
No nostalgia
No softness
No fondness on which to reminisce
Just red hot flares blazing into smoke
Emotion stifles the flames
In that fire
We must find ourselves

Dear Sister,

We often put ourselves straight into the fire. The old saying of "out of the frying pan and into the fire" is how we seem to live our lives. Often, however, it is in the fire in which we find ourselves. Through our trials and tribulations, our bad and worse times these are the flames that will allow us to rise up from as we should be. We will find ourselves through the process.

But that doesn't mean that the fire has to be hot enough to turn us to ash before we rise...

Finding yourself in the fire means that you have realized that you no longer want to live with that which you have lived with at this point. It means that you are ready to rise above the flames and come into your Self. You are no longer willing to cherish memories of the past which don't serve you in the present. There's nothing nostalgic or worthy of reminiscing in the flames. We let our emotions get in the way and sometimes the flames are cooled off and we stay, thinking things will be better. But when the red hot flares begin blazing again, we must -- we MUST -- rise above and be born anew.

Points to Ponder

The birth of anything doesn't come with ease. Animals labor to deliver their young as do us Two-Leggeds. Birthing your dream, your Authentic Self, is no different. As the baby's head leaves the birth canal, the intense pain is called "the ring of fire" but out of that fire comes the delicate sweetness of new life. Give birth to yourself today through the ring of fire you now sit within.

Alchemical Art Journaling

Giving birth to anything is no easy process. Today we will "give birth" to our Authentic Self. For this, you will need the following supplies:

Your Journal
Black Cardstock
Circle Template
Red/Orange/Yellow Paint Markers
A Photo of Yourself (one you really like; it can be a copy)
White Paint Marker (Fine/Bullet nib)

Purge

On a blank page in your journal, write down all the things that you've "lost in the fire" -- those things which you no longer cherish. Throw it into the fire with "no nostalgia, no softness, no fondness on which to reminisce." It is no longer needed, no longer wanted. You are looking instead at finding yourself -- at being reborn through the flames. So feed the fire with the pain and heartbreak of the past. Write it all down. This is fuel for the fire which you will be birthed from.

Meditation Moment

Light your candle and take a sip of tea. Settle in to a comfy position in a chair or on the floor. This time, I want you to focus your attention on the flame of the fire from the candle. Watch its dance, its flicker, its grace. Lean into the feelings that come up as you watch the flame's flicker. Empty all of your thoughts into the fire and watch the dance it does in its consumption of the fuel you are feeding it. Lean into the dance from the flickering flame and envision yourself dancing up out of the fire, being reborn. Now rise to your feet and dance without inhibition. Sway to and fro like the dance of the candle flame. As you are dancing, call for your rebirth. Announce out loud that you are doing the Dance of Your Rebirth and allow all shackles and restraints to fall from your former self in order that you may dance to the rhythm of your heart sounds. When you feel a wash of newness come over you, yell out "Thank You!" to the Divine who has allowed your rebirth. Welcome back!

Paint

Cut the black cardstock down to the size of your page then cut a large circle in the center using your circle template. Take your paint markers and paint rings of flames around the circle, symbolizing the "ring of fire" women experience during childbirth. Allow the paint to dry fully.

Produce

Adhere the picture of yourself to the back of the black cardstock such that it shows through the whole/ring of fire. You are being reborn through this symbolic ring.

Integrate

Now, adhere this to your page on top of your writings of what you lost in the fire. Integrate these things that you have shed into the new you as you are being reborn. Allow what serves you to become part of you and give thanks as you are releasing that which no longer serves you.

LYRICAL JOURNEY

CRUCIFY me UPSIDE DOWN just so that i can maybe feel a part of my own world again, even if its only when it comes to my religion.

You unleashed your tempestuous violence on me, and began PUTTING THE DAMAGE ON until i was shattered, BODY AND SOUL.

Now, it is WINTER, the perfect season to bring the heat of judgment to my moon risen days.

My eyes go SNOWBLIND as i watch the DARK SIDE OF THE SUN descend, while the tides rise on their WAY DOWN...

So yes, CRUCIFY me UPSIDE DOWN, just like the Antichrist that i have become.

Claim me please, FATHER LUCIFER, i can be your LADY IN BLUE, your OPHELIA... ... .

I am now a stranger, lost in my own world.

You stole my purity and filled me with darkness...will the sun ever ascend again for me? Or am i caught eternally in THE CHASE, in your cat and mouse game where every nightfall its the NIGHT OF HUNTERS?

Only time will tell, but for now, I am feeding your demon seed, slowly becoming a jaded version of a PLAYBOY MOMMY.

Its too late to reclaim my holiness.

Never even came close to becoming a MRS.JESUS, now i may be fated to always remain a Magdalene...forever lost among the MARYS OF THE SEA of confusion u have tried to drown me in. You overwhelm every aspect of my life. My BODY AND SOUL. You are even HERE. IN MY HEAD, as i am speaking to you.

Your seed swims within me, through PANDORA'S AQUARIUM, which is housed inside my soul...its splicing each reef of memory ive grown through time, and experience..

These cherished memories that you mercilessly are now causing to fade, casting them down from their vibrant rainbow hues, to a melancholy monochrome with your 16 SHADES OF BLUE.

Each brush stroke has turned to flesh cuts as i stumble through your FOREST OF GLASS, and this SWEET SANGRIA of my crimson blood flows from me, as though trying to purge my sins borne of you, yet no matter how long i bleed, you still course strongly through my veins with unabashed FEARLESSNESS....

Turning the tides of this SHATTERING SEA, I stand poised amidst the AMBER WAVES, and i pray UNDER THE PINK moon, asking for forgiveness from the FATHERS SON....
"GOD, what will it take for me to just feel human again?"

My sanctity has been desecrated by this STRONG BLACK VINE that you have twisted and bound me with....

You have diluted my world.

You are Hades and i am Demeter after u took my Persephone...the world is much colder now....

And i wonder...

What will it take?

It's as if my sacrifice was insufficient for these DEVILS AND GODS, and i must continue to walk this earth alone, seeking my redemption...

I must repent for this act you violently commited on me, an uninvited display of ORIGINAL SINSUALITY i was an unwilling participant in...

Yet in trying to escape that perpetual sorrow, I've instead lost my way...but i havent completely lost myself,at least not yet....

Somewhere amidst the darkness there is a TWINKLE of hope..that perhaps this is not the end, and even in the eye of this soulquake i can have faith that i am NOT DYING TODAY..

I can still hold onto the belief that somewhere inside me, exists the goddess i know i am, and always have been...

For all women, we all of us are goddesses, and as the recipients of blame in this patriarchy we must grow out of our shame, into a sisterhood of UNREPENTANT GERALDINES...proud and unapologetic.

Show this misogynistic patriarchy what a real MOTHER REVOLUTION looks like..

And i slowly begin to realize i must not surrender to my sorrow, because even in my darkest moments, my personal Hell is sadly ANOTHER GIRL'S PARADISE....so instead now i pray for you, my dark passenger, my captor.....you who has preyed upon my innocence, because you can only feel strong by being ABNORMALLY ATTRACTED TO SIN, crossing the threshold of humanly flawed to eternally unforgiven...but even in this fragile state you have broken me into...i find compassion..

Compassion not only for you, but for myself.
Although at times i may feel inside like i am another tragic story of a GIRL DISAPPEARING, i know i am not alone...how many others have there been? Its for them i must forge ahead. They have suffered, SILENT ALL THESE YEARS, and now i will be their voice.

You crashed into my world all fury and rage, right when it was peaceful, perfect, and ALMOST ROSEY...and obliterated my only haven i ever knew..

but i forgive you.

You took my purity, enslaved me, made me walk through your broken FOREST OF GLASS which gave me scars i will bear for a lifetime.

And I forgive you.

You think you won...simply because you've broken pieces of me temporarily
But broken will heal and I am NOT DYING TODAY...

Instead, from the devastation, i rise..transformed. Heart and spirit weakened, but yet i still stand before you;
broken but not defeated.

I have arisen.

Like a phoenix.

I am a goddess.

But most of all..

I am a survivor.

And I. Will. live.

Dear Sister,
We have arrived at the end of our journey together, which is really just the beginning…

We have travelled the path of 12 different journeys, arriving together at this point right here. We have realized that "somewhere inside [of us], exists the goddess [we] know [we are], and always have been…" And now it is time.

For all women, we all of us are goddesses, and as the recipients of blame in this patriarchy we must grow out of our shame, into a sisterhood of UNREPENTANT GERALDINES…proud and unapologetic.

Show this misogynistic patriarchy what a real MOTHER REVOLUTION looks like…"

And that, Dear Sister, is where your journey begins. It begins by showing all those that would rather see you kept "in your place", all those who strove to put you down and keep you there that you are the captain of your vessel.. Do not surrender to sorrow. Do not allow shame and blame to get the best of you. Forgive yourself and then forgive those which must be forgiven in order for you to complete the healing process. Be compassionate – to Self first and then to others. Know that you are not alone in this world or along your journey. There are always sisters there to cast you a guiding light.

Yes – forgive, for forgiveness is not for the trespasser, it is for you! Without forgiveness only bitterness will abide. Don't give free space in your head to the likes of bitterness… It is your time to rise transformed. You may be broken but know that you are NOT defeated! You have been reborn through the fire, you have danced in its flames, you have transcended the ring and have manifested yourself anew. Now go out into the world and show your Self that from this moment forward you will only live Authentically!

Points to Ponder

The only thing left to ponder is how wholly will you allow the work in this book to transcend into your being and become one with your Spirit? You were given 12 activities to assist you in purging the muck and mire and integrating only that which serves you. How will you apply those lessons in your life going forward? What will you manifest for your Self – your Authentic Self?

Alchemical Art Journaling

The steps we've taken thus far of Purging, Meditating, Painting, Producing, and Integrating were done in order that at this point, you would have bite size chunks from the roadmap of using art intentionally in order to heal your Self. This is the launching pad for all of the work you have done prior to this point. Now it is your turn to launch. It is your turn to purge that which this poem, Lyrical Journey, brings up for you. It is your turn to paint the colors of your Self onto the canvas of your life.

Although there is no guided activity for this last poem, there is guidance in the poem and its message. Sit with it for a while and then pull your journal out. Allow the whisperings of your heart to guide the activities on the pages before you. In the end, write a prayer. One which encompasses all that you have transcended during this journey in conversation with me, your Sister, and which integrates all that you have learned from this volume into your Self.

ABOUT THE AUTHOR

"A. Friend" is the pen name for the Visionary Artist, Sumaiyah Dymonz Yates. Her pen name is a play on her middle and maiden names (Anne Friend thus A. Friend) because she wants her writing to always come from "a friend." Ms. Friend is a Certified Intentional Creativity Coach, Certified Spiritual Coach, and a Certified Color of Woman Teacher. She has taken wisdom gained through personal experience along with the professional training she has received and produced this volume as a gentle way to introduce using intentional creativity in your life, rather than diving in head strong as the work of intentional creativity as a tool for healing can be intense. Ms. Friend has been published in the Red Thread Nation Leadership Circle, is a Contributing Writer for Mother of Nurture, and a regular Guest Host on A Year in the Life of an Art Journal. She has also appeared in various other publications which appear both in print and online. Ms. Friend (Sumaiyah Yates) is also the owner and founder of the Soulful Emergence Art Gallery, located in Baltimore, Maryland. This is a full-service art gallery which is currently representing 10 female artists located

around the world. Lastly, she has recently launched Transcendental WINGS: Women Intent on Nurturing the Goddess pSyche – a community of women who gather together for sisterhood, creativity, wisdom circles, Girls' Night Out, and more.

To learn more about Ms. Friend and her work writing and using intentional creativity (art journaling, painting, and mixed media) as tools for healing, she can be contacted using any of the following methods:

Artist Website: www.Simply-Sumaiyah.com
Online Community: www.Transcendental-WINGS.com
Art Gallery Website: www.Soulful-Emergence.org
Facebook: https://www.facebook.com/simply.sumaiyah
Twitter: @SoulfulEmergnce
Pinterest: http://www.pinterest.com/soulfulemergnce/

A. FRIEND

www.ingramcontent.com/pod-product-compliance
Lightning Source LLC
Chambersburg PA
CBHW051709090426
42736CB00013B/2622